Poisoned Rivers and Lakes

by Ellen Lawrence

Consultants:

Daniel L. Ceynar
The Iowa Flood Center, IIHR Hydroscience & Engineering
The University of Iowa, Iowa City, Iowa

Kimberly Brenneman, PhD
National Institute for Early Education Research, Rutgers University
New Brunswick, New Jersey

BEARPORT
PUBLISHING

New York, New York

Credits

Cover, © chriscrowley/iStock/Thinkstock and © Boris Khamitsevich/iStock/Thinkstock; 2–3, © Pierre Crom/Photoshot; 4–5, © Robert Harding Specialist Stock/Corbis; 6, © Mike Kahn/Green Stock Media; 7T, © Creative Commons Public Domain; 7, © Wayne Hutchinson/FLPA; 8–9, © xpixel/Shutterstock; 10–11, © Craig Stephen/Alamy, © AlinaMD/Shutterstock, © mycola/Shutterstock, © Sergey Goruppa/Shutterstock, and © Sergey Dubrovskiy/iStock/Thinkstock; 12, © Darley Shen/Corbis; 13, © Santia/Shutterstock; 14, © fluke samed/Shutterstock; 15, © Jose B. Ruiz/Nature Picture Library; 16, © euroluftbild/Glowimages; 17, © UbjsP/Shutterstock; 18–19, © Laura K. Roberts/Iowa River Clean-up, Iowa City, Iowa; 20, © Marie-Françoise Hatte/Deerfield River Watershed Association; 21TL, © Monkey Business Images/Shutterstock; 21BL, © Moreno Soppelsa/Shutterstock; 21TR, © photobank.ch/Shutterstock and © Matt Valentine/Shutterstock; 21BR, © Monkey Business Images/Shutterstock; 22, © Sergey Goruppa/Shutterstock and © artzenter/Shutterstock; 23L, © Portokalis/Shutterstock; 23TR, © RTImages/Shutterstock; 23BR, © Laura K. Roberts/Iowa River Clean-up, Iowa City, Iowa.

Publisher: Kenn Goin
Editor: Jessica Rudolph
Creative Director: Spencer Brinker
Design: Emma Randall
Photo Researcher: Ruby Tuesday Books Ltd

Library of Congress Cataloging-in-Publication Data in process at time of publication (2014)
Library of Congress Control Number: 2013043670
ISBN-13: 978-1-62724-105-2 (library binding)

For more information, write to Bearport Publishing Company, Inc., 45 West 21st Street, Suite 3B, New York, New York 10010. Printed in the United States of America.

10 9 8 7 6 5 4 3 2 1

Contents

A Polluted Home

A swan searches for plants and insects to eat in a river.

However, it's hard for the bird to find food.

That's because there's so much trash in the water.

Trash isn't the only **pollution** that's spoiling the swan's river home.

The water also contains other pollution that can't even be seen!

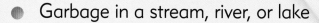

Garbage in a stream, river, or lake might include food containers, cans, and plastic bottles. Large items, such as tires and supermarket carts, sometimes end up in the water as well.

a swan looking for food in a river

What kinds of trash can you see in this picture? How do you think the trash got into the water?

Harmful Trash

How does trash get into streams, rivers, and lakes?

Sometimes, people dump it into the water or drop it from a boat.

Other times, people leave litter on the ground and the wind blows it into the water.

Fish, birds, and other animals often eat the trash because they think it's food.

Eating garbage can make animals very sick—and even kill them!

storm drain

Rain can wash trash left on the street down a **storm drain**. Then the trash is carried by rainwater through underground pipes into a stream, river, or lake.

Animals can also get tangled in trash.

garbage dumped near a river

Poisonous Water

Chemicals are another type of pollution that can harm rivers and lakes.

Sometimes, factories dump chemicals, such as those used to make paint and glue, into rivers.

If animals swallow this polluted water, they can be **poisoned**.

Sometimes, people pour oil and harmful chemicals down storm drains. These poisonous liquids can end up in streams, rivers, and lakes.

fish killed by chemicals in a river

Chemicals from Farms

Chemicals used to help **crops** grow can also end up in rivers and lakes.

After the chemicals are sprayed onto crops, they soak into the ground.

Then they can trickle into nearby streams, rivers, and lakes.

In the water, these chemicals help tiny living things called **algae** grow.

More algae grow until a thick layer of slime called an algae bloom covers the water.

Unfortunately, the algae can cause a river great harm.

1 A tractor sprays chemicals onto crops.

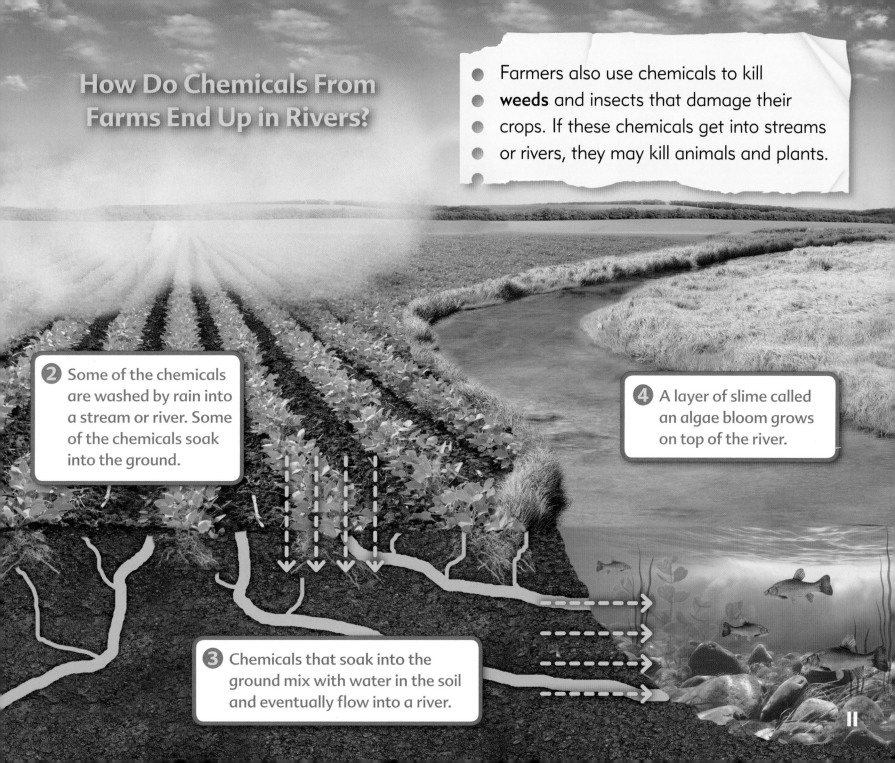

How Do Chemicals From Farms End Up in Rivers?

Farmers also use chemicals to kill **weeds** and insects that damage their crops. If these chemicals get into streams or rivers, they may kill animals and plants.

2 Some of the chemicals are washed by rain into a stream or river. Some of the chemicals soak into the ground.

4 A layer of slime called an algae bloom grows on top of the river.

3 Chemicals that soak into the ground mix with water in the soil and eventually flow into a river.

Dangerous Slime

An algae bloom is harmful to plants and animals in the river.

The slime blocks out sunlight that underwater plants need to grow.

If the plants die, animals that eat the plants won't have food.

Algae blooms can also use up all the **oxygen** in the water.

Then there is no oxygen left for fish and other underwater animals to breathe.

a dead fish floating in algae

- Animals that live on land use lungs to breathe oxygen from the air. Underwater animals, such as fish, use body parts called gills to breathe oxygen that's in the water.

a river turned green by an algae bloom

Pollution in rivers can end up in the ocean. How do you think this happens?

From Stream to Ocean

Pollution in streams and rivers can reach the ocean. How?

A person might dump trash or chemicals into a small stream.

The stream then flows into a larger river, bringing the pollution with it.

Once the pollution is in a river, it will be carried out to sea.

That's because all rivers eventually flow into the ocean.

a crab covered in oil

Just like animals that live in rivers and lakes, ocean animals, such as fish, turtles, crabs, and seabirds, can be harmed by trash, chemicals, and oil that get into the water.

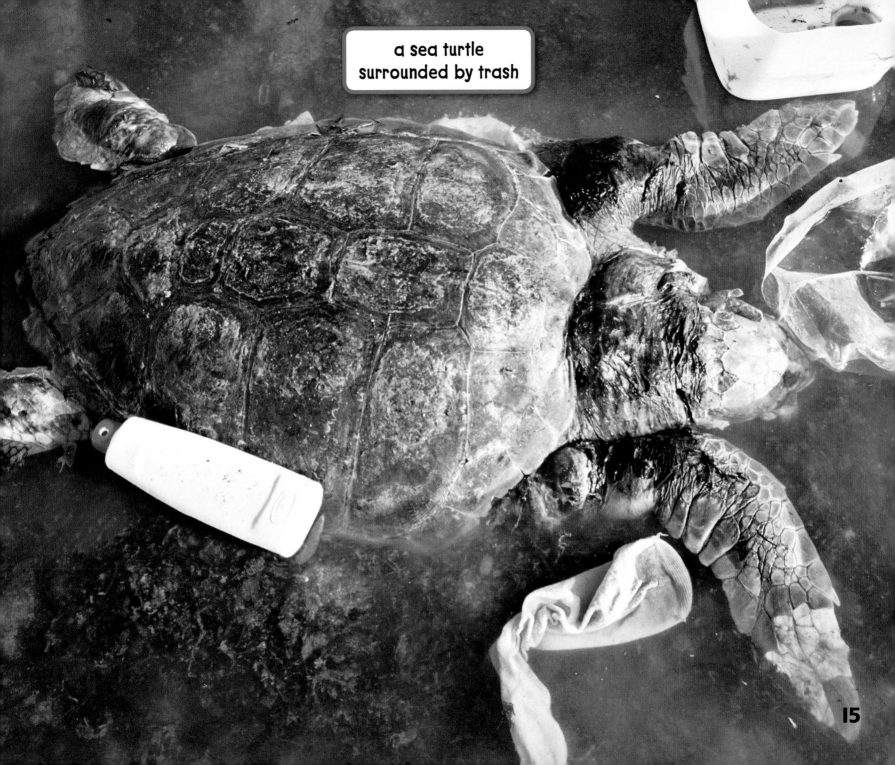

a sea turtle surrounded by trash

Stop the Pollution!

Streams, rivers, and lakes are home to thousands of kinds of animals and plants.

They are also places where people swim, boat, and fish.

So it's important for people to protect these places.

Farmers should stop using harmful chemicals on their crops.

Factories should never dump chemicals into rivers or lakes.

a water treatment plant

Much of the water that people drink comes from rivers and lakes. The water is **purified**, or cleaned, at water treatment plants so it is safe to drink.

a beaver family
living in a river

River Cleanup

Some people help clean up dirty rivers.

Like many rivers, the Iowa River gets polluted with lots of trash.

Once every year, **volunteers** in Iowa spend a day removing trash from the water.

Some volunteers paddle along the river, collecting trash in boats.

The trash is then **recycled** or taken to a **landfill**.

During the 2013 Iowa River cleanup, volunteers removed 200 old tires from the water. The total amount of trash collected weighed as much as two elephants!

volunteers picking up trash in the Iowa River

What can you do to help keep rivers and lakes safe from pollution?

Everyone Can Help

There are many ways to help keep streams, rivers, and lakes clean.

For example, never drop trash on the ground.

The trash could be washed down a storm drain or get blown into a river or lake.

Being careful with your trash helps keep rivers, lakes, and even oceans clean for the future!

Some people help keep rivers clean by painting signs near storm drains. The signs tell people not to dump chemicals or other pollution into the drains.

What Can You Do?

Here are some ways to stop pollution from getting into rivers and lakes.

Recycle Your Trash

If you visit a river or lake, take your trash home and recycle it or throw it in the garbage.

Put paper, plastic bottles, aluminum cans, and glass bottles and jars into a recycling bin.

The items will be taken to special factories, where they will be turned into new items.

crushed plastic bottles at a recycling factory

Stop Chemical Pollution

Tell adults to never pour paint or oil down storm drains.

You can also tell adults not to use chemicals to kill weeds in their yards. Just as on farms, these chemicals can soak into the ground. Then they might find their way into streams or lakes.

Science Lab

Be a Clean Water Champion!

Animals, plants, and people need clean water to live and stay healthy. However, many rivers, lakes, and oceans are being damaged by pollution. Make a poster to tell your friends and family about this problem. Your poster can also tell people what they can do to help.

You will need:

- Construction paper
- Paint, colored pencils, or markers
- Scissors
- Glue
- Pictures from old magazines or printed from the Internet

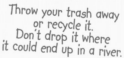

STOP **Polluting Our Water**

Pollution damages rivers, lakes, and oceans.

Animals eat plastic trash and die.

Chemicals poison animals.

Throw your trash away or recycle it. Don't drop it where it could end up in a river.

Never pour paint or oil down a storm drain.

> You can draw pictures on your poster.

> You can cut out pictures from old magazines.

> Ask an adult to help you find pictures online and print them.

Science Words

algae (AL-jee) tiny plant-like living things that grow in water

chemicals (KEM-uh-kuhlz) natural or human-made substances that can sometimes be harmful to living things

crops (KROPS) plants that are grown on farms, usually for food

landfill (LAND-fill) a large hole in the ground where garbage is dumped and buried

oxygen (OK-suh-juhn) a colorless gas that is found in the air and water, which animals and people need to breathe

poisoned (POI-zuhnd) killed or hurt by eating or drinking a harmful substance

pollution (puh-LOO-shuhn) materials, such as trash and chemicals, that can damage the air, water, or soil

purified (PYOOR-uh-fyed) having dirt, chemicals, and other unwanted substances removed from something to make it clean

recycled (ree-SYE-kuhld) when used, old, and unwanted objects are turned into something new

storm drain (STORM DRAYN) a hole in the ground, usually covered with a metal grill; rainwater runs into a drain and flows through underground pipes until it empties into a river, a lake, or an ocean

volunteers (vol-uhn-TIHRZ) people who do work without pay to help others

weeds (WEEDZ) plants that grow where they are not wanted; most weeds are very tough and fast-growing and can prevent other plants from growing

Index

Read More

Goodman, Polly. *Rivers in Danger (Earth Alert!).* New York: Gareth Stevens (2012).

Mason, Paul. *Rivers Under Threat (World in Peril).* Chicago: Heinemann (2009).

Learn More Online

To learn more about polluted rivers and lakes, visit
www.bearportpublishing.com/GreenWorldCleanWorld

About the Author

Ellen Lawrence lives in the United Kingdom. Her favorite books to write are those about nature and animals. In fact, the first book Ellen bought for herself, when she was six years old, was the story of a gorilla named Patty Cake that was born in New York's Central Park Zoo.